Cecilia McDowall

Bird of Time

for soprano solo, SSATB, and piano
or small ensemble

vocal score

OXFORD
UNIVERSITY PRESS

OXFORD
UNIVERSITY PRESS

Great Clarendon Street, Oxford OX2 6DP,
United Kingdom

Oxford University Press is a department of the University of Oxford.
It furthers the University's objective of excellence in research, scholarship,
and education by publishing worldwide. Oxford is a registered trade mark of
Oxford University Press in the UK and in certain other countries

First published 2025

Impression: 1

ISBN 978–0–19–357732–9

Music origination by Anna Williams
Text origination by Katie Johnston

Printed in Great Britain on acid-free paper

Contents

Composer's note   iv

Texts   v

1. The Bird of Time   1
2. Aubade (a lament)   15
3. To Be Bird   21

Duration: 15 minutes

Instrumentation

oboe
percussion—1 player (glockenspiel, vibraphone, suspended cymbal, tambourine)
strings

Full scores and instrumental parts are available on hire/rental.

If required, the work may also be accompanied by piano, playing from the vocal score.

Composer's note

On receiving this special commission from Ealing Choral Society to celebrate their sixtieth anniversary, I was keen to involve the choir in some way. I asked the singers to share some suggestions of poetic texts, to see where they took me. There were many texts I loved among them, but there was one poem in particular that fascinated me, submitted by the treasurer, Cynthia Haliburn: 'The Bird of Time' by the remarkable Indian political activist, feminist, and poet, Sarojini Naidu. And it seemed especially apposite to be setting her poetry in 2022, the seventy-fifth anniversary year of Indian independence.

Following the pandemic, I think we have become more alive to what we hold most dear. With restrictions imposed on our day-to-day activities in lockdown, many of us took to exercising in the streets. There were few cars, no overhead planes, and in the silence we heard … the birdsong: exquisitely beautiful, full of variety, and loud! And it is the idea of this precious sound that is at the heart of this cantata.

The text for the first movement, Sarojini Naidu's poem embraces sorrow, loss, and hope for the future. Each verse asks the 'Bird of Time' a question: 'What are the songs you sing?' In the lines that follow, we learn of such poignant contrasts, of joy and despair, of dreams and laughter, of life and death. The movement closes by restating the opening couplet. Life's full circle, perhaps.

Growing up in the sixties I was very aware of the influence that the book *Silent Spring*, by marine biologist and conservationist Rachel Carson, had on my parents. I can even remember the arresting look of the book with a dead bird on the cover. The second movement, 'Aubade', for soprano solo and chorus, is a setting of a poem by Seán Street. Seán and I have collaborated many times before and it is always a joy to share ideas and work together. I have subtitled Seán's poem 'a lament'. The soprano soloist opens the movement, singing of the dawn chorus which we hear 'out of darkness, song before flight … dawn song before everything'. The chorus then picks up the phrase 'out of darkness'. In the second verse the soprano intimates that the avian population is dwindling; this time the chorus sings 'into darkness'. In the last verse, 'silent spring' has arrived with its 'haunting silence beyond repair'; the chorus responds, 'beyond darkness'.

In the last movement, 'To Be Bird', we now have a bird's-eye view of how we humans might appear to these airborne creatures. And they are not impressed! When we discussed how this poem might be, Seán related how he had heard, during the pandemic when planes were a rare thing, a nestful of startled chicks squawking at the sudden rush of sound from an aeroplane. In the second verse Seán conjures up some indignation at such a disturbance. The final verse accepts that humans are hopeless: 'You aspire to be bird? Oh my word, it's absurd!'

First performed by Ealing Choral Society, with Orpheus Sinfonia and Danni O'Neill, soprano, conducted by Peter Asprey, at St Barnabas Church, Ealing, London, on 12 November 2022.

This note may be reproduced as required for programme notes.

Texts

These texts may be reproduced as required for programme notes.

1. The Bird of Time

O Bird of Time on your fruitful bough
What are the songs you sing? …
Songs of the glory and gladness of life,
Of poignant sorrow and passionate strife,
And the lilting joy of the spring;
Of hope that sows for the years unborn,
And faith that dreams of a tarrying morn,
The fragrant peace of the twilight's breath,
And the mystic silence that men call death.

O Bird of Time, say where did you learn
The changing measures you sing? …
In blowing forests and breaking tides,
In the happy laughter of new-made brides,
And the nests of the new-born spring;
In the dawn that thrills to a mother's prayer,
And the night that shelters a heart's despair,
In the sigh of pity, the sob of hate,
And the pride of a soul that has conquered fate.

Sarojini Naidu (1879–1949)

2. Aubade

Air made audible.
Out of darkness,
song before flight, before wing,
dawn song before everything.
Out of darkness.

A music maker
for those who sang,
for the diminishing choir,
less in each unfeathering hour.
Into darkness.

Absence visible,
and morning song
haunting silence beyond repair,
filling space where their voices were.
Beyond darkness.

Seán Street (b. 1946)
© Seán Street 2025. Reproduced by kind permission of the author.

3. To Be Bird

You aspire to be bird,
beyond word into song,
beyond earth into sky,
but ground makes your sound
too solid, too rooted
to be part of our choir.

Your thunder and roar,
the noise as you soar,
disturbing our night,
clouding our light,
drowning out our protests,
and the joy of our nests.

Were you as we, you'd see
how to grow into blue.
We are not here for you
but ourselves, so how can
we teach you the sky,
teach you transparency?
You aspire to be bird?
Oh my word, it's absurd!

Seán Street (b. 1946)

Commissioned by Ealing Choral Society on the occasion of their 60th anniversary

Bird of Time

CECILIA McDOWALL

1. The Bird of Time

Sarojini Naidu (1879–1949)

OXFORD UNIVERSITY PRESS, MUSIC DEPARTMENT, GREAT CLARENDON STREET, OXFORD OX2 6DP

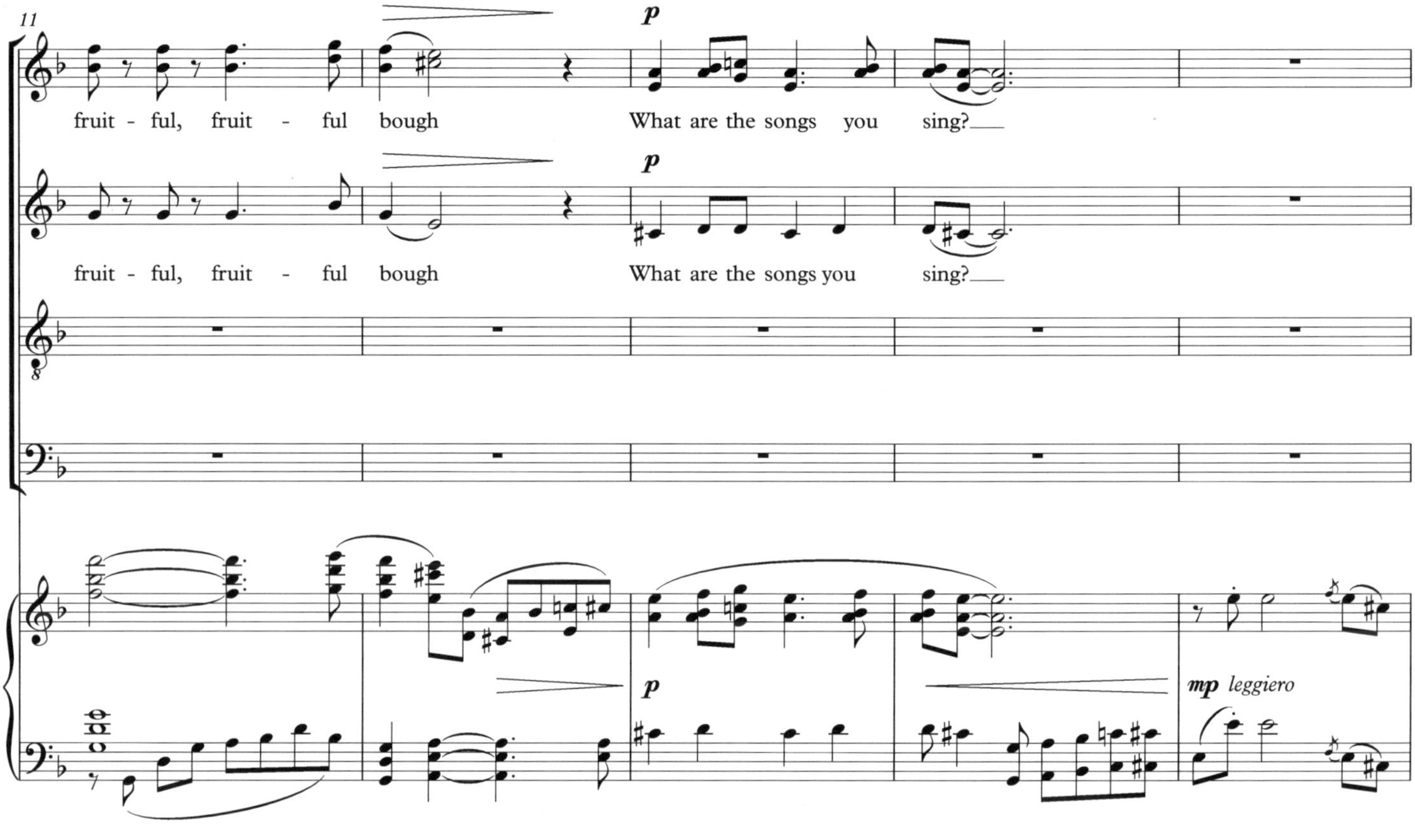
11
p
fruit - ful, fruit - ful bough
What are the songs you sing?
p
fruit - ful, fruit - ful bough
What are the songs you sing?
p
mp leggiero

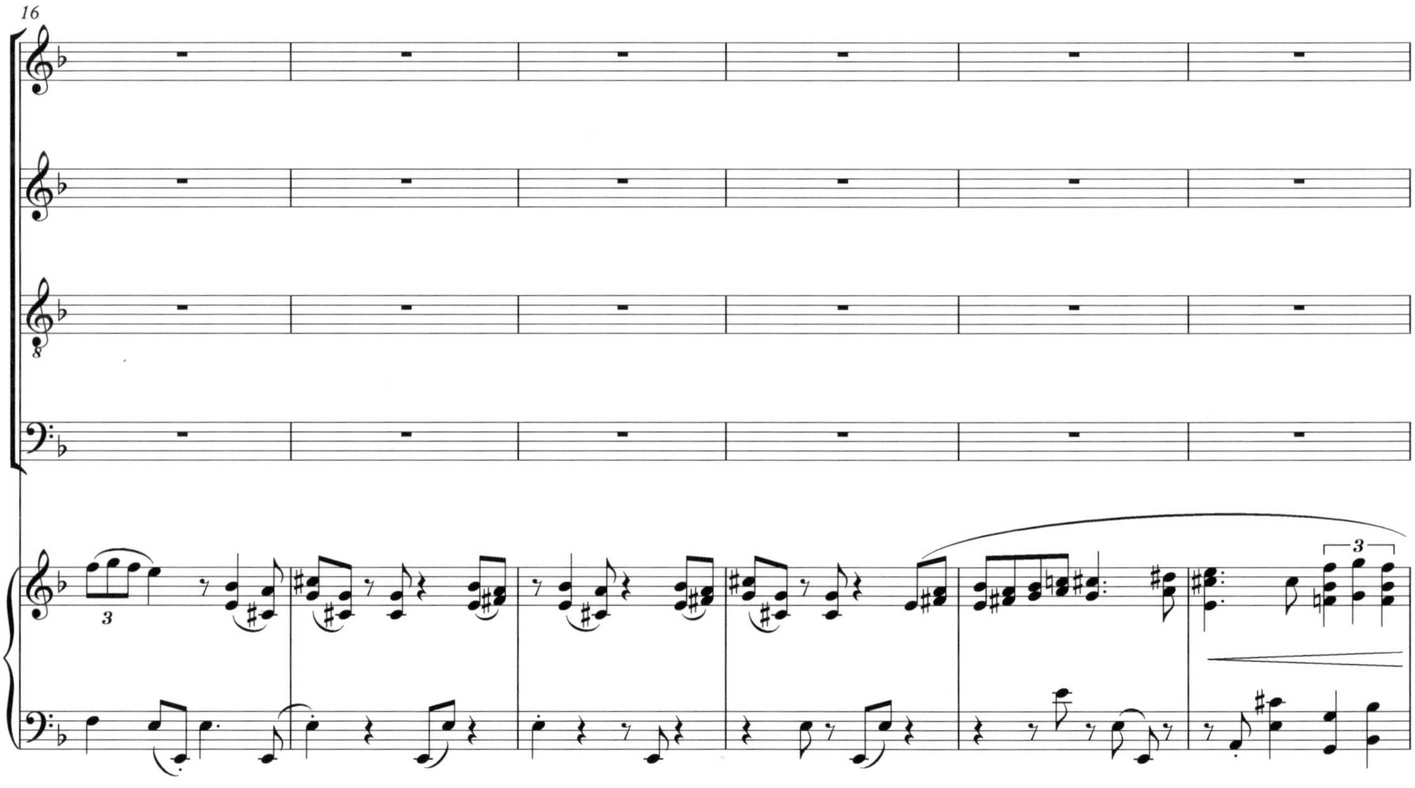
16
3
3

What are the songs you sing?

What are the songs you sing?

What are the songs you sing?

What are the songs you sing?

espressivo e cantabile

poco rit.

poco rit.

2. Aubade (a lament)

Seán Street (b. 1946)

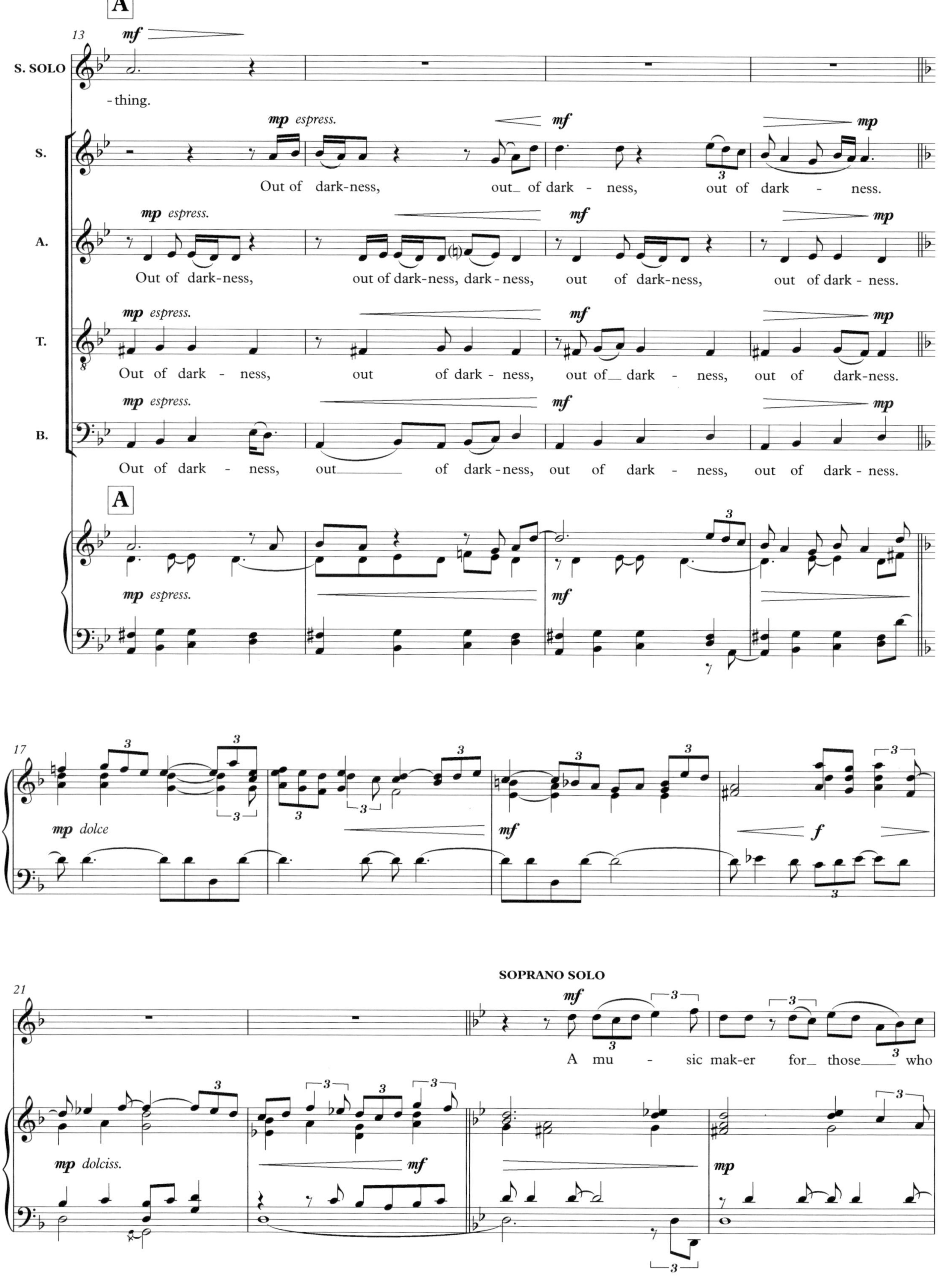

A

S. SOLO
-thing.

S.
Out of dark-ness, out of dark - ness, out of dark - ness.

A.
Out of dark-ness, out of dark-ness, dark-ness, out of dark-ness, out of dark - ness.

T.
Out of dark - ness, out of dark - ness, out of dark - ness, out of dark-ness.

B.
Out of dark - ness, out of dark-ness, out of dark - ness, out of dark - ness.

A

SOPRANO SOLO

A mu - sic mak-er for those who

3. To Be Bird

Seán Street (b. 1946)

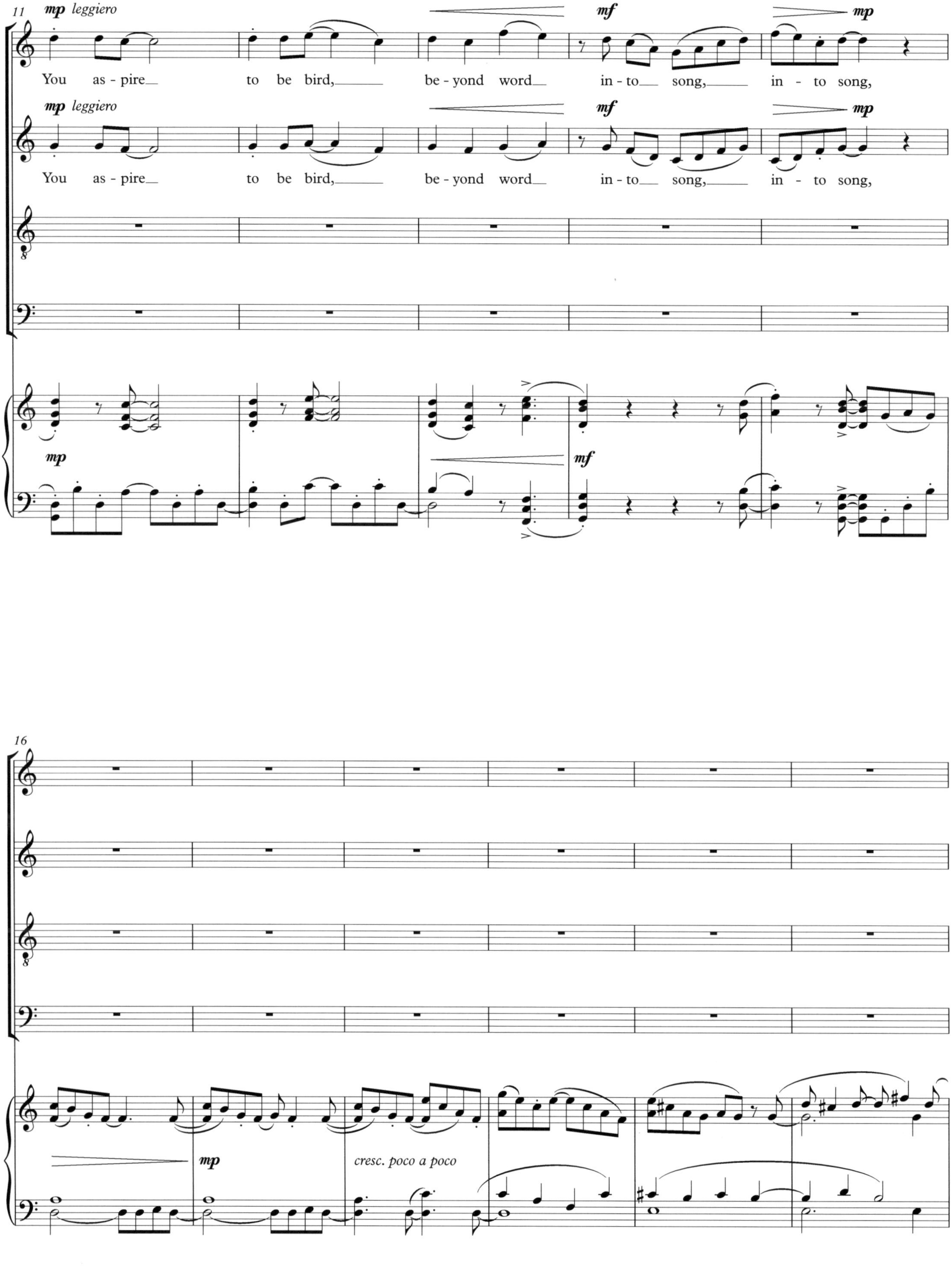
11
mp leggiero
You aspire to be bird, be-yond word in-to song, in - to song,
mf
mp
mp leggiero
You as-pire to be bird, be-yond word in-to song, in - to song,
mf
mp
mp
mf
16
mp
cresc. poco a poco

A
22
mf
be - yond earth
in - to sky,
f
but
too so-lid, too root-ed,
so-lid, root-ed,
so-lid, root-ed, but
27
leggiero
ground makes your sound
too so - lid, root-ed,
so - lid, root-ed

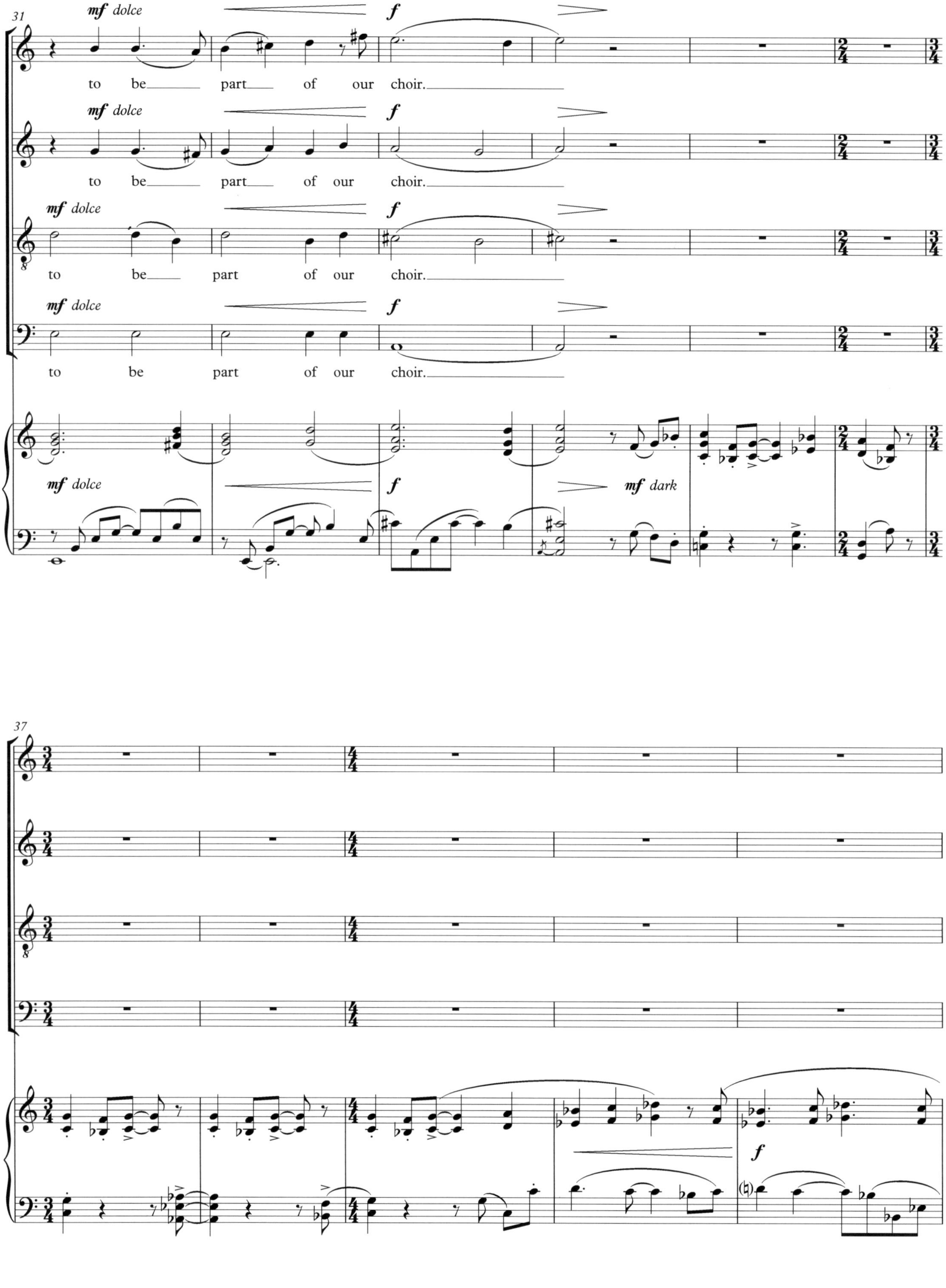
31
mf dolce
f
to be part of our choir.
mf dolce
f
to be part of our choir.
mf dolce
f
to be part of our choir.
mf dolce
f
to be part of our choir.
mf dolce
f
mf dark
37
f

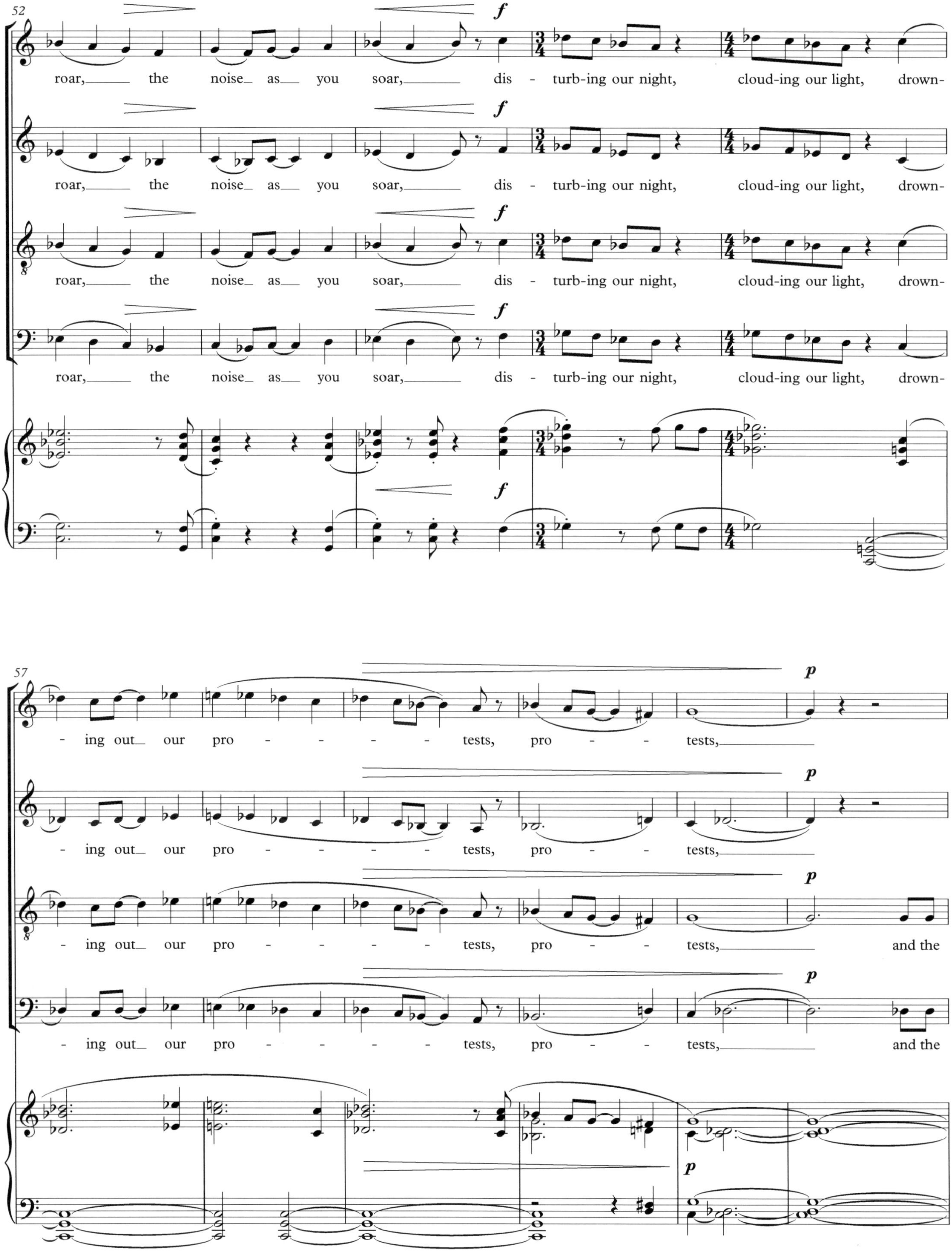
52
f
roar, the noise as you soar, dis - turb-ing our night, cloud-ing our light, drown-
57
p
- ing out our pro - - - - tests, pro - - - tests,
and the